Net Brennan

SPORTSMANSHIP

How sport shaped Australia

black dog

For Warwick, Jas, Nate and Josh.

The author would like to thank Alistair Scott and Dean Bird for their input, as well as the talented team at Black Dog Books, particularly Maryann Ballantyne, Nicola Santilli and Amy Daoud.

The author and publisher thank Marion Littlejohn and Dr Brian Wimborne for their thorough expert read of Sportsmanship.

First published in 2016 by ✈ black dog books, an imprint of Walker Books Australia Pty Ltd
Locked Bag 22, Newtown, NSW 2042 Australia | www.walkerbooks.com.au

National Library of Australia Cataloguing-in-Publication entry:
Brennan, Janette, author.
Sportsmanship / Janette Brennan.
ISBN: 978 1 742032 33 7 (paperback)
Series: Our stories.
For children.
Subjects: Sportsmanship – Australia. Professionalism in sports – Australia. Sports – Moral and ethical aspects – Australia. Aboriginal Australians – Sports. Women athletes – Australia.
796.0994

Typeset in Bembo | Printed and bound in China | 10 9 8 7 6 5 4 3 2 1

IMAGE CREDITS: **Front cover, p6** Group portrait of cricket team, c. 1905–c. 1910, SLV; **Front cover, p18** John Landy c. 1954, SLV; **Front cover, p22** Arthur Beetson looks for a teammate before passing the ball, NLA; **Front cover, p24** The America's Cup, Wikimedia Commons; **Back cover, p1, p15** Cricket field background © Shutterstock.com/N.Minton; **p1, p18, p28** Red running track stock image © Shutterstock.com/Awirut Somsanguan; **p1, p20** Background of rippled pattern of clean water in blue swimming pool © Shutterstock.com/mehmetcan; **p1, p30** Sisters Booka and Chris Durack sparring with a speed bag, 1916, SLQ; **p2, p3** The finish for the Melbourne Cup, 1881, SLV; **p4** Aboriginal cricket team and Tom Wills, 1866, Wikimedia Commons; **p4, p12** Grass stock image © Flickr.com/eh3k, under a Creative Commons 2.0 license; **p5** Sketches at the football match – Geelong v. Melbourne, 1880, SLV; **p7** Melbourne Cup Winners Australia 1861–1902 (Archer), Melbourne Cup crowd, 1889, SLV; **p8** Death of English Cricket, Wikimedia Commons; Ashes Urn © Flickr.com/danielgreef, under a Creative Commons 2.0 license; **p9** Portrait of Fanny Durack, 1912, NLA; **p10** Soldiers playing cricket, Green Shell, Gallipoli, Turkey, December 1915, SLV; **p11** Les Darcy, SLNSW; Sportsmen's Thousand posters, SLV; **p12** Phar Lap c. 1930, SLV; **p13** How Phar Lap finished in the Melbourne Cup Race, 5th November, 1930, SLV; **p14** Don Bradman at practice, SLNSW; **p16** Harold Larwood strikes Bert Oldfield in the head with a bouncer, 16 January 1933 © H H Fishwick/Fairfax Syndication; **p17** Don Bradman with his "Don Bradman" brand Sykes bat, SLNSW; Cricket ball stock photo © Shutterstock.com/untitled; **p19** Portrait of Betty Cuthbert, NLA; Shirley Strickland in the women's 80 metres hurdle final, Olympic Games, Melbourne Cricket Ground, Victoria, 1956 © News Ltd/Newspix; **p20** Dawn Fraser in the 100 metres freestyle final at the Olympic pool, Melbourne, 1956 © Bruce Howard/Newspix; **p21** Shane Gould, 1971, National Archives of Australia: A1500, K26030; **p23** Norm Provan (St George) and Arthur Summons (Wests) leave a muddy SCG after the 1963 Rugby League Grand Final © John O'Gready/Fairfax Syndication; **p23, p27** Soccer Field stock image © Shutterstock.com/antpkr; **p25** *Australia II* © 1983 Larry Moran; **p26** Nicky Winmar points to his skin in response to a racist taunt from the crowd, April 1993 © Wayne Ludbey/Fairfax Syndication; **p27** St Kilda's Nicky Winmar during his 200th AFL game, the St Kilda v. Brisbane match, 27 July 1997 © Joe Armao/Fairfax Syndication; **p28** Cathy Freeman at the Sydney Olympic games, 25 September 2000 © Pat Scala/Fairfax Syndication; **p29** Dawn Fraser, Cathy Freeman, Shane Gould, Raelene Boyle and Betty Cuthbert, 15 September 2000 © Andrew Zakeli/Fairfax Syndication.

Contents

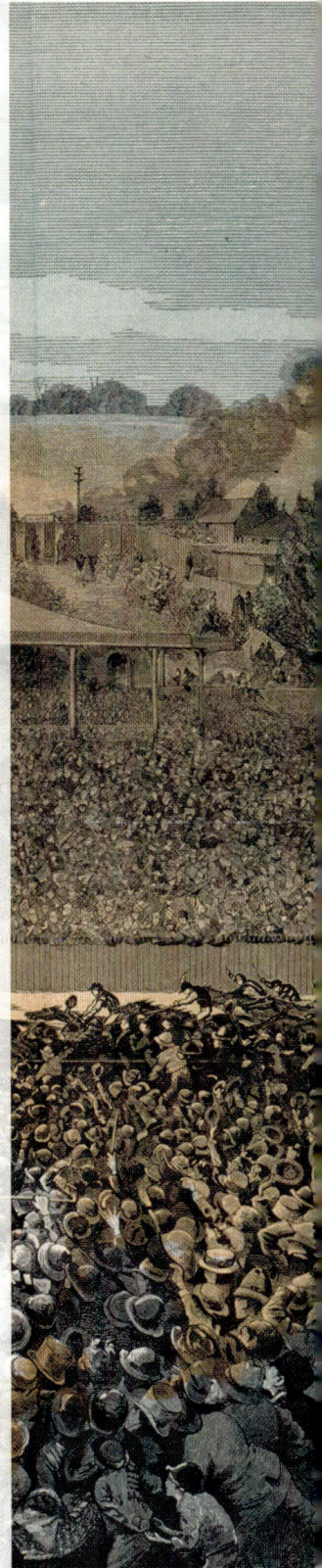

In the Beginning, There was Cricket

In 1880, a schoolteacher named James F Hogan warned that future Australians would have three main "defects": a larrikin spirit, a dislike of mental effort and an inordinate love of sports. Hogan claimed that nine out of every ten people born in Australia spent "all their leisure in the practice of either cricket or football". He blamed the sunny weather for this obsession.

Hogan made this prediction close to 100 years after the British, in 1788, established a penal colony in New South Wales (NSW). The 1880s was an interesting era because it was the first time since European settlement that Australian-born colonists outnumbered immigrants. People were beginning to wonder if a distinctive Australian identity was developing, and sport was one of the ways they defined and tested this local character.

Sport has given Australia some of its greatest memories, and these legends reflect our history and our values. Sport has also created one of the few things in the world that is unique to Australia … and it all began with a bored cricketer.

The first Australian cricket team with coach and captain Tom Wills, 1866

Australia's Game

Australia was a cricket team before it was a nation. A group of talented Aboriginal players toured England in 1868, more than 30 years before the Federation of Australia. These athletic cricketers from Victoria's Western Districts delighted thousands of English fans on their 47-match tour.

The first captain/coach of the Aboriginal cricket team was a non-Indigenous man called Thomas Wentworth "Tom" Wills. He was the greatest Australian cricketer of his time. Wills was the grandson of convicts who'd made good in Australia. Sent as a teenager to an English boarding school called Rugby, Wills struggled as a student but excelled at cricket and football. At the time, footy had any number of players, and rules that were made up before every match.

"Let go the ball"

The Melbourne and Geelong footy clubs (pictured) were among the first to join Wills's competition. The "Demons" and "Cats" were formed in 1858 and 1859 respectively, making them two of the oldest football clubs in the world.

Wills returned to Australia in 1856 and joined the Victorian cricket team for its second-ever match against NSW. These two colonies were fierce rivals: NSW was the first European settlement and considered itself "Number One" while Victoria, very rich after the gold rushes of the 1850s, viewed itself as simply superior. The intercolonial cricket matches were seen as a chance to prove which "society" truly was best. During this match it was NSW, but Wills soon became the Victorian captain and led his colony to many wins.

The First Laws of Football

On 10 July 1858, Wills published a letter in a newspaper called *Bell's Life in Victoria*. He wrote that cricketers were getting a bit chubby during winter and suggested that they organise a football club to draw up a set of rules. The following month, advertisements appeared in the local papers: on Saturday, 7 August, a game of football would be played on Richmond Paddock (now known as Yarra Park), just outside the area that is now the Melbourne Cricket Ground (MCG). Forty Scotch College boys would oppose a similar number from Melbourne Grammar School, and Wills would be one of the two umpires. There were no fixed rules, and tripping, elbowing and tackling were all part of the game. The match was played over three Saturdays and each team scored a goal. Some parents complained about the violence, but most people wanted more.

On 17 May 1859, Wills met with some friends at the Parade Hotel near Richmond Paddock and wrote down 10 rules for the new Melbourne code of football. These rules banned hacking (kicking in the shins), described the act of taking a mark (catching the ball directly from a kick) and stated that the ball could never be thrown.

The rules written by Wills and his friends that day were some of the first official laws for any football code in the world.

Many seasons have since passed but even today, Wills is never far from the big game. A statue outside the MCG, on the site of the 1858 footy match, depicts Wills umpiring two young players. The inscription on the statue says Wills "did more than any other person – as a footballer and umpire, co-writer of the rules and promoter of the game – to develop Australian football during its first decade".

In the 1800s, Aboriginal men were seen playing big kicking games similar to today's Australian football. The best known of these was called *marngrook*. Tom Wills was brought up in north-western Victoria and would have known of these games, if not played them. Perhaps marngrook was the inspiration for Australian football. No-one knows for sure.

Colonial "Pie-oneers"

An English immigrant named William Francis King was famous in Sydney in the 1830s and 1840s for selling "fast" food. His food was fast because he would offer hot pies to locals as they boarded the Parramatta ferry, then run more than 25 kilometres to offer more pies to the same passengers as they disembarked. The legend of "The Ladies' Walking Flying Pieman" gradually grew legs, and so did King's hunger to perform even crazier acts of pedestrianism.

The Flying Pieman twice beat a horse-drawn mail coach in a race between Sydney and Windsor (close to 60 kilometres), carried a fat dog from Campbelltown to Sydney (around 55 kilometres) and beat the Brisbane to Ipswich mail coach by an hour while carrying a heavy pole (more than 40 kilometres). In his most famous event, The Flying Pieman boasted he could walk 1000 quarter miles (402 kilometres) in 1000 quarter hours (roughly 10 days). He placed a coffin beside the track and had himself horse-whipped for motivation.

Throwing Like a Girl

In the early 1800s, an Englishwoman named Christina Willes invented cricket's roundarm bowling. The hoop at the bottom of her long skirt meant she couldn't bowl underarm, the way the best cricketers bowled at the time, so she tried bowling over her shoulder. Willes's action quickly became popular and, in 1835, it was included in cricket's official rules.

The place of women in sport was not as eagerly embraced. Within the Australian colonies there were women who could, for instance, ride a horse as well as any man, such as Ellen Kelly, the mother of the bushranger Ned Kelly. But physical exertion was not considered ladylike. One of the reasons sport was said to be bad for women was because it took them away from their housework – the same argument that was used at the time for why women should not be allowed to vote. A little golf, tennis or croquet was socially acceptable for women, as long as they didn't try too hard.

Women's cricket team, c. 1905-1910

The Race that Stops a Nation

There's a legend that a racehorse named Archer walked more than 800 kilometres to win the first Melbourne Cup. Archer supposedly walked this distance because there wasn't a rail link between his home in Nowra, NSW, and Flemington, Victoria. This story is doubted now because newspapers from the time mentioned Archer's journey to Melbourne by ship. Either way, Archer went on to beat the favourites by six lengths in a race that saw two horses die, another bolt off the course and two jockeys injured in falls.

Around 4000 people attended the 1861 Melbourne Cup, which was well below the 20,000-plus who had flocked to an earlier Victorian race meeting. One of the reasons for the disappointing turnout was that Melbournians had just learned of the deaths of beloved outback explorers Robert O'Hara Burke and William John Wills, and were in mourning.

Archer, winner of the first two Melbourne Cup races

Archer returned to win the second Melbourne Cup in 1862, when the event was starting to become a popular carnival. By the 1880s, crowds of 100,000-plus (more than a third of Melbourne's population) regularly flocked to Flemington for the sideshows, the picnics, the fashion – and the horses.

Archer's record of two consecutive Cup wins went unbroken for more than 100 years.

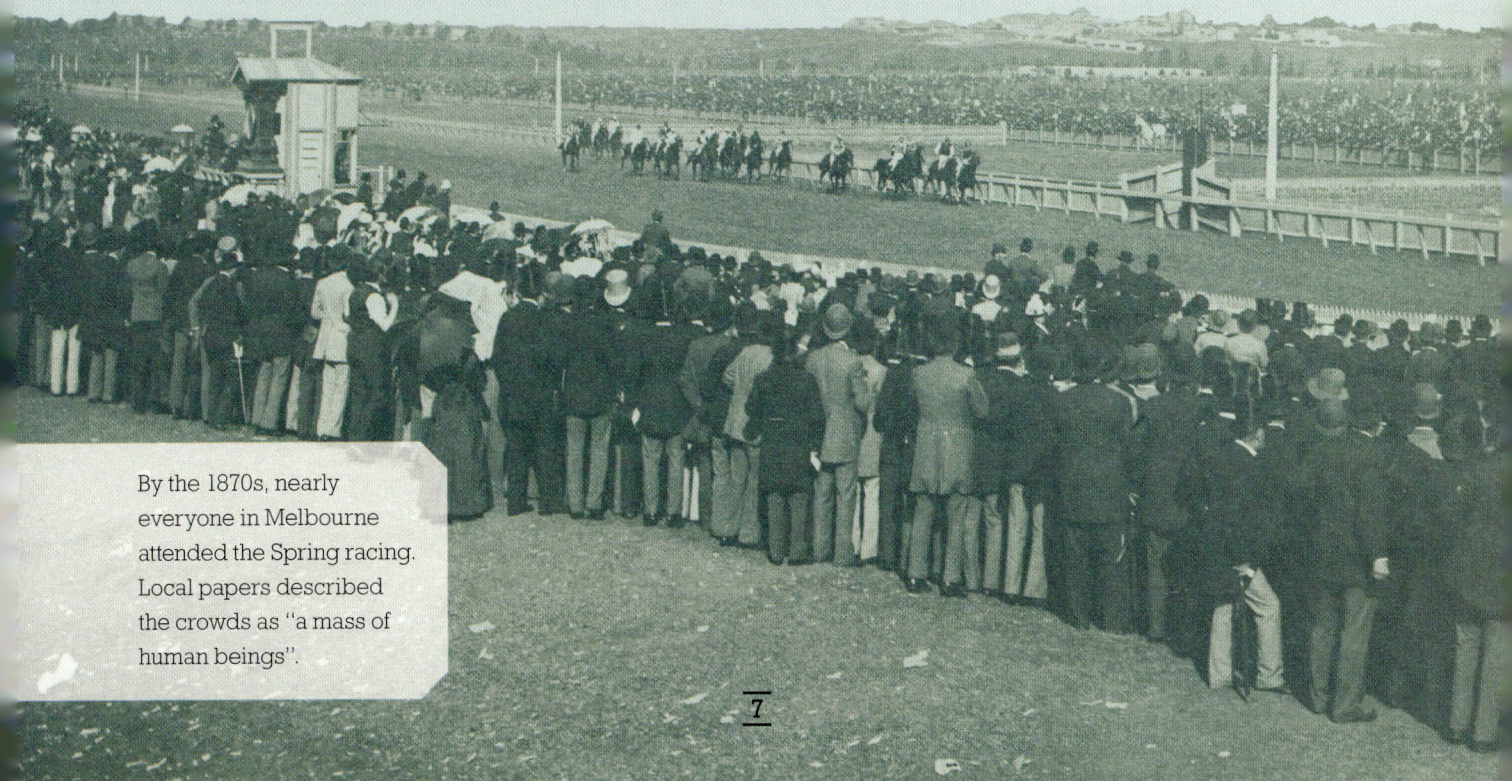

By the 1870s, nearly everyone in Melbourne attended the Spring racing. Local papers described the crowds as "a mass of human beings".

The Ashes

In 1882, this notice appeared in a British newspaper to mourn the death of English cricket. It was a joke by a journalist who, days before, had watched Australia beat a full-strength English team on English soil for the first time ever. The "Poms" had looked unbeatable until they were cut down by the pace of an Australian bowler named Fred "The Demon" Spofforth. One English fan at the ground died of a heart attack, several others fainted and another was so shocked by England's batting collapse that he bit through the handle of his umbrella. Several weeks later, the English team set sail for a cricket tour of the Australian colonies. Before boarding the ship, the captain, Ivo Bligh, promised to bring back "the ashes of English cricket", although no actual trophy existed at this time. The newspapers loved Bligh's reference to the Ashes and reported it widely.

In Affectionate Remembrance
OF
ENGLISH CRICKET,
WHICH DIED AT THE OVAL
ON
29th AUGUST, 1882,
Deeply lamented by a large circle of sorrowing friends and acquaintances.

— R.I.P. —

N.B.—The body will be cremated and the ashes taken to Australia.

"Death" of English cricket, from *The Sporting Times London*, 2 September 1882

Bowling a Maiden Over

After arriving in Australia, Bligh and several members of his team were invited to spend Christmas at the estate of millionaire Sir William Clarke. On Christmas Day the English cricketers played a social match against the locals. As a joke, Lady Janet Clarke, the wife of Sir William, and her friend Florence Morphy, burned some of the bails, placed the ashes into a small clay urn (possibly an empty perfume bottle) and presented it to Bligh. Glued to the front of the 11-centimetre-tall urn was a label that said "THE ASHES".

In the following weeks the English team won the Test series 2–1. Bligh also won the heart of Florence Morphy – they married in February 1884. The Ashes urn sat in the Bligh's home for the next 43 years. Florence eventually donated it to the Marylebone Cricket Club Museum at Lord's, the spiritual home of cricket, following her husband's death. It is extremely rare for the urn to be taken from the museum, even though Australia and England usually battle for the Ashes every two years.

Olympic Originals

An accountant from Victoria named Edwin Flack was our first Olympic champion. He travelled to Athens in 1896 to watch the first Olympic Games of the modern era and, at the last minute, decided to enter the 1500-metres and 800-metres running races. He won both. He even had a go at the marathon and led for much of the event, before collapsing at around the 34-kilometre mark.

Flack's victories were so popular that he was chosen to lead the parade of athletes at the Closing Ceremony. His decision to compete in 1896 helped establish Australia as one of the few nations to have competed in every modern Summer Olympics.

"They tell me that I have become the Lion of Athens."
EDWIN FLACK, 1896

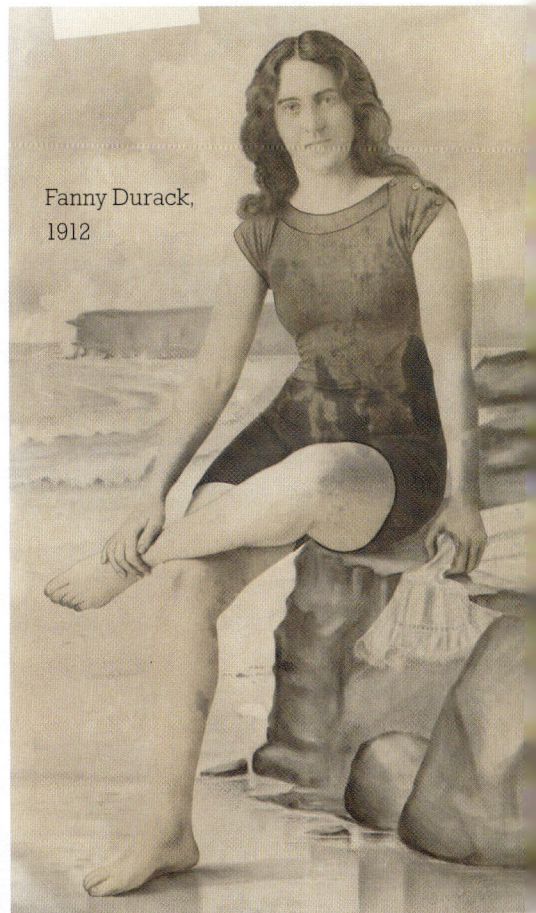

Making a Splash

One hundred years ago, this photo may have offended you. Sydney swimmer Sarah "Fanny" Durack was the first woman in the world to win Olympic swimming gold, but the toughest opposition for Durack did not come from the pool. Instead it came from Australian officials who said Durack's woollen swimming costume, like the one she is wearing in this picture, was too brief to be seen in public.

A decade or so earlier the newly-Federated Commonwealth of Australia had given women both the right to vote and to stand for federal parliament. But life remained difficult for women swimmers because many community leaders felt it was wrong for them to wear such revealing outfits.

So, for the sake of modesty, Durack was not initially included in the Australian team for the 1912 Stockholm Olympics, where a women's swimming race was included for the first time. Eventually public outcry forced the team officials to back down. Durack went on to win the 100-metres final in a world record time. It was the start of a golden tradition for Australian women at the Olympics, particularly in the pool.

Fanny Durack, 1912

The Fighting Spirit

On 17 December 1915, Australian soldiers played a game of cricket among the trenches. It was the final days of the Gallipoli campaign in World War I (WWI) and the Allied forces (from nations such as Australia, Britain, France and New Zealand) were leaving the Turkish peninsula. The eight-month campaign had been a failure, so thousands of soldiers were secretly being evacuated in the hope that no more lives would be lost. The orders went out that the last remaining men should create a distraction, and that's when a group of diggers decided to play a game of cricket. Their "pitch" was on a flat patch of dirt called Shell Green, so named because it was under constant fire.

After a couple of hours the Turks got bored with watching the cricket and started firing at the Australians. It was extremely dangerous but the diggers treated it as a big joke. They even pretended to field some of the shells before stumps were called and the game declared a draw.

More than 60,000 Australians were killed in WWI while fighting in Gallipoli, Western Europe and the Middle East. In 2001, to honour the spirit and sacrifice of these original Anzacs, the Australian cricket team visited Shell Green and recreated the original picture.

Australian and New Zealand forces first landed in Gallipoli, Turkey, on 25 April 1915. That date is now commemorated each year as Anzac Day.

Soldiers playing cricket on Shell Green, Gallipoli, Turkey, 1915

The Tragedy of Les Darcy

James Leslie "Les" Darcy began winning fights and fans when he was fourteen. He won the Australian middleweight title while still a teenager and then knocked out a much bigger opponent to claim the heavyweight crown.

The Australian public loved Darcy because he didn't drink, smoke or swear. And since his elder brother was disabled and his father unemployed, Darcy gave all of his prize money to his family. Even his opponents admired him and said Darcy was hard to hit and harder still to hurt. But Darcy could be hurt.

Australia entered WWI in 1914. Thousands of Australian sons, fathers and brothers were laying down their lives and this made people wonder whether the proper place for Australia's greatest fighter was in the trenches. Darcy began to receive white feathers, a symbol of cowardice, which wounded him deeply.

Darcy tried to enlist, but he needed his parents' permission because he was younger than twenty-one. His mother refused to sign his enlistment papers. Darcy became the target of the angry debate about whether the government should force men to fight. The power to do this is called conscription and the first of two referendums, asking Australians whether it should be introduced, was held in 1916.

The day before this referendum, and several days before Darcy's 21st birthday, the boxer snuck aboard a boat headed for the United States. Darcy said he planned only a handful of American fights, just enough to look after his family, before he would do his duty as a soldier. Back in Australia, the newspapers branded Darcy a coward.

The bad press followed Darcy to the States. When his first fight was promoted in New York, the local governor stepped in and banned the "shirker". Another fight was organised in another city, only to again have it stopped by officials. It happened over and over. The pressure began to take its toll. Darcy developed a persistent cough and a sore throat. Feeling weak, he was admitted to hospital, but didn't recover. Infection spread throughout his body and, several weeks later, the champ was dead.

It is estimated that 700,000 people lined the streets of Sydney when Darcy's body was returned for burial.

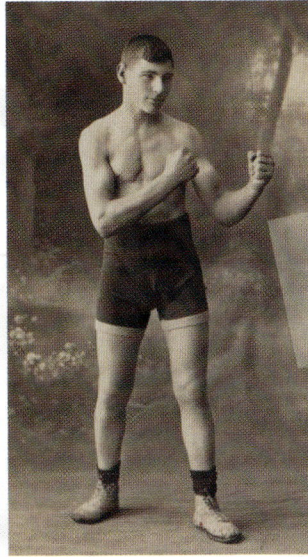

Les Darcy, c. 1909–1917

Play THE Game!

These enlistment posters from WWI show how Australia's passion for sport was used to encourage men to become soldiers. These sorts of posters told men to "Play up! Play THE game!" – a line from a famous poem about a dutiful cricketer who became a dutiful soldier. Lieutenant Albert Jacka is in the middle. He was the first Australian in WWI to win the Victoria Cross, the highest military award for acts of bravery.

The Wonder Horse

At sunrise on 1 November 1930, a shotgun was fired from a car at a racehorse returning from training. The horse's carer leapt in front of the animal to protect it and both were lucky to escape unhurt. That horse was Phar Lap, his brave carer was Aaron Treve "Tommy" Woodcock, and the following seven days witnessed the making of an Australian legend.

Why would someone want to shoot Phar Lap? It was probably to do with money. When Phar Lap was just a colt, he looked something like a half-starved kangaroo with giraffe legs. Everyone thought he was worthless, except Woodcock and the horse's trainer, Harry Telford. They were right. By the time Phar Lap was three, he was becoming muscular, tall and almost unbeatable on the track. But Phar Lap's success was bad for the people who bet on his rivals. No one was ever charged over the shooting, although it was probably the act of a punter who wanted the wonder horse out of the way.

The plan to shoot Phar Lap backfired. Several hours after the attempt on his life, Phar Lap easily won the Melbourne Stakes. Three days later he stormed home to claim the 1930 Melbourne Cup. Two days after that he was first past the post in the Linlithgow Stakes, and the following Saturday he was victorious in the CB Fisher Plate. Phar Lap had won 14 races in a row around this time, so his week of victories at the Flemington spring carnival was no surprise. It is, however, a feat that will probably never be repeated.

Phar Lap, c. 1930

Phar Lap winning the Melbourne Cup Race, 1930

You Can Bank on Phar Lap

Phar Lap's rise from humble beginnings made him a hero for every Australian who was doing it tough – and in the 1930s, there were a lot of them. This era is called the Great Depression because it was a time when many people lost their jobs, and families became homeless. But as banks went broke, Phar Lap broke records. Australians across the nation enjoyed his victories through cinema newsreels, household wirelesses and daily newspapers, which were all starting to become popular.

After winning nearly everything there was to win in Australia, Phar Lap was taken to the United States to race against the best horses in the world. The first start was at a track on the Mexican side of the American border and Phar Lap smashed the rest of the field. This victory had a huge impact: Phar Lap received movie offers from Hollywood producers, and even a message of congratulations from King George V.

> Phar Lap means "lightning" in the Thai language.

Was He Poisoned?

On the morning of 5 April 1932, Woodcock noticed that Phar Lap showed signs of colic, a stomach condition common in horses. A veterinarian was called but Phar Lap's temperature soared and he groaned in pain. Woodcock guided Phar Lap into his stall. The champ fell to the floor and rested his head in Woodcock's lap. Moments later, Phar Lap passed away.

"HE IS DEAD" was the headline in nearly every newspaper across Australia. There were lots of reports and rumours that Phar Lap hadn't died from colic but from a disease, bad food, an infection, or poisoning – perhaps accidental, perhaps deliberate. Tommy Woodcock wrestled with these questions for the rest of his life. Even today, there still isn't a clear answer.

Phar Lap continues to be the people's champion. His stuffed hide is the most popular exhibit at the Melbourne Museum and his heart, almost twice the size of other horses, is displayed at the National Museum of Australia in Canberra. If someone shows great courage or spirit, Australians often say they have "a heart as big as Phar Lap's".

Bodyline

Don Bradman at practice, 1932

ir Donald George "Don" Bradman was nearly twice as good as any other cricketer who has ever swung a bat. The boy from Bowral, NSW, had a Test average of 99.94 in a sport where the best of the rest average in the high 50s.

Bradman could trace his passion for cricket back to the age of twelve when he was taken to a Test Match at the Sydney Cricket Ground (SCG). "I shall never be satisfied," he told his father, "until I have played on this ground". Within seven years Bradman had claimed a century in his first game for NSW and then, aged twenty-one, he broke the world batting record by scoring 452 runs against Queensland.

Later that year, Bradman joined the 1930 Australian Tour of England and scored a double century in his first game on English soil. He destroyed opposition bowling with steel-hard concentration, sweetly timed shots and quick-fire scoring. By the end of the tour "The Don" had collected 2960 runs, including six double centuries and a Test record score of 334, of which 309 runs were in a single day.

Bradman was the first celebrity superstar of Australian sport and could not be stopped. Or could he?

Hour after hour, a young Don Bradman perfected his batting skills by using a cricket stump to hit a golf ball against the base of his backyard water tank.

Fast Leg Theory

The man selected to captain England for the 1932–33 Ashes Tour of Australia was Douglas Jardine. He was a clever cricketer, best known for his ruthless will to win. Jardine studied film of Bradman's batting to search for a weakness and was told of a moment on the 1930 tour when the Australian had flinched against a fast, rising delivery.

"I've got it," Jardine said as he replayed the Bradman footage. "He's yellow." Jardine was convinced that Bradman was scared of fast bowling, even though The Don scored 232 runs in that particular game.

So a plan was hatched called fast leg theory. Under this strategy the bowler would target the body of the batsman. Meanwhile, the fielders – crowding in a ring around the leg side, or the area behind the batsman – would snap up catches as the batsman tried to defend himself. England's tactic depended on bowlers who were lightning quick and deadly accurate, and a coal miner named Harold Larwood was perfect for the task.

"There are two teams out there but only one of them is playing cricket."

AUSTRALIAN CAPTAIN BILL WOODFULL, 1933

It's Just Not Cricket

Jardine's team launched fast leg theory bowling in the opening matches of their Ashes tour, belting the Australian batsmen black and blue. The hurt felt by the Australians was deeper than simple bruising. The tactics of bowling on the line of the body – or bodyline, as the newspapers called it – may not have been completely against the laws of cricket at the time, but it was far from the standards expected of the English. Cricket, after all, was supposed to be a game played by gentlemen.

England easily won the first Test and there was talk in the Australian dressing room of fighting back with their own bodyline tactics. The Australian captain, William "Bill" Woodfull, didn't want anything to do with it. Woodfull was a school principal as well as a man of great principle. He refused to stoop to England's level.

A century by Bradman in the second Test raised hopes that Australia might find a way to rise above bodyline bowling. At the same time the Aussie players, who normally batted with little more than gloves and leg pads, started making their own protective gear to strap across their chests, arms and thighs.

Adelaide Erupts

In January 1933, the English and Australian teams travelled to Adelaide and the third Test got underway. Harold Larwood was as explosive as ever – he could bowl three times faster than the speed that a modern car drives along suburban streets. Late in the afternoon on the second day, one of his deliveries hit Woodfull over the heart. The Australian captain dropped his bat, clutched his chest and staggered off the pitch. Meanwhile, as Woodfull doubled over in agony, Jardine called out to his bowler: "Well bowled."

When Woodfull faced his next delivery, England's fielders formed a bodyline ring around him. Woodfull was peppered, ball after ball, with deliveries that thumped all over his body. The fans at the ground could not believe their eyes. Men, women and children jumped to their feet to scream and yell and boo as the England bowlers ripped through the Australian batting line-up.

Later it was the turn of Bert Oldfield, the Australian wicketkeeper, to face Larwood. One of Larwood's deliveries bounced off the pitch and hit Oldfield in the right temple, fracturing his skull. The wound was only centimetres from a steel plate that Oldfield received when injured by an exploding shell in WWI. As Oldfield was led from the field, blood streaming from his forehead, hundreds of police officers moved into position, fearing a riot. In the end the Adelaide crowd did not storm the pitch. England went on to win this match, as well as the Ashes series, 4–1. Bradman, the main target of bodyline, was restricted to the single century.

English bowler Harold Larwood strikes Australian wicketkeeper Bert Oldfield in the head with a bouncer, 16 January 1933

Who'd You Call a Cheat?

Australian cricket officials complained about bodyline to the sport's governing body in England. They described it as "unsportsmanlike" and said that unless it stopped, it would "upset the friendly relations existing between Australia and England".

The word "unsportsmanlike" annoyed English officials. They demanded an apology. This stand-off risked more than the future of cricket: tensions were also felt at a government level, where whispers were heard about bans to trade.

In the end, no official action was taken against bodyline until it was later used in England. On 21 November 1934, almost two years after fast leg theory was first unleashed in Australia, laws were put in place to curb dangerous bowling. Today, batsmen are better protected from bodyline tactics by fielding and bowling restrictions – as well as helmets.

The Real War

Bradman went on to become captain of the Australian team and, in the 15 years of his career following bodyline, he lost only four Test matches to England. These battles faded into the background from 1939 to 1945 when the world was again engulfed by a real war. Almost a million Australian men and women served in World War II (WWII). This number included 500,000 who fought against Germany and Italy in Europe, North Africa and the Mediterranean, as well as those who battled the Japanese in south-east Asia and the Pacific. The mainland of Australia also came under attack with bombing raids on the north and north-west of the continent (including Darwin) and enemy submarines in Sydney Harbour.

Don Bradman with his "Don Bradman" Sykes bat, c. 1932

Invincible

Three years after the end of WWII, Bradman led his final tour of England. Fifteen of the players in the 17-man squad were former servicemen. That 1948 team went through the entire tour undefeated. They are remembered as the Invincibles.

Don Bradman died in 2001, aged ninety-two. He had been the last surviving player of the bodyline series. Even after his retirement from cricket, Bradman received hundreds of letters every week from fans all over the world. It's said he personally replied to them all. At the time of the cricketer's death the then-prime minister, John Howard, described Bradman as the most remarkable Australian of the past 100 years.

Hosting the World

During the 1956 Australian National Championship for the mile (1.6 kilometres), a runner named John Landy stopped mid-race to help a fallen rival. Landy had been behind Ron Clarke when Clarke clipped the heels of another competitor and fell to the ground. Landy tried to hurdle Clarke but the spikes of his shoes cut into the youngster's shoulder and arm. Unselfishly, Landy stopped, ran back towards Clarke with an outstretched arm and apologised. "Get going," Clarke yelled back, and that's exactly what Landy did.

There were fewer than two laps left in the race and the frontrunners had opened a gap of around 40 metres. Landy's giant strides helped him to catch and overtake the leaders one by one. Then, urged on by the frenzied crowd, Landy unleashed a final sprint that won him the National Championship and created Australian folklore.

At the time of this race, Landy was one of only two men in the world who had run a mile in under four minutes. This was a big, big deal. Previously people had wondered if it was even possible for the human body to be pushed fast enough for long enough to break the four-minute barrier. Some thought runners would die if they even tried.

Landy's fame around the world as a champion distance runner was used to promote the 1956 Melbourne Games, the first-ever Olympics held in the Southern Hemisphere. Landy was given the honour of taking the Olympic Oath on behalf of the 3300 athletes. Nineteen-year-old Clarke, who later set many world records, lit the Olympic Flame within the stadium.

John Landy, c. 1954

Golden Girls of the Games

The Melbourne Olympic Games were a chance to show the world that the Australian nation was growing up. Competing against 72 nations in 17 sports, Australia finished third on the medal tally with 13 gold, 8 silver and 14 bronze. That's the best Australia had ever placed.

Only 46 of the 325 athletes in the Australian team were women, and they won 7 of Australia's 13 gold medals. Eighteen-year-old sprinter Elizabeth "Betty" Cuthbert led this charge. A gifted and hardworking athlete, Cuthbert was known for running with her mouth open. It meant she sometimes swallowed flies, but it didn't slow her down. Cuthbert became the golden girl of the Games when she won the 100-metres and 200-metres sprint double, and anchored Australia's world-record-breaking relay team.

Hurdler Shirley Strickland de la Hunty also ran in that winning relay team, giving her a combined tally of seven medals from the 1948, 1952 and 1956 Olympics. This total remains one of the best-ever Olympic records by an Australian. Despite de la Hunty's track record, some people hadn't expected her to compete at the Melbourne Games simply because she was a thirty-one-year-old mother. Ideas about what women were capable of doing had changed during WWII, when they filled "men's jobs" in factories, on farms and in the armed forces. After WWII, women were encouraged to surrender these jobs to returned soldiers. By the 1950s, a married woman like de la Hunty was expected to devote her life to her husband, her children and her housework – not a sporting career.

Betty Cuthbert

Shirley Strickland, 1956

One Olympic Nation

The 1956 Melbourne Games was the first time the athletes walked together in the Closing Ceremony as one Olympic nation. This display of unity is different to the Opening Ceremony, in which the athletes march in separate teams behind their country's flag. The idea to create a combined group of athletes was suggested by an Australian-born schoolboy of Chinese descent called John Ian Wing. He wanted the Closing Ceremony to encourage togetherness. This gesture has since become an Olympic tradition and is one of the reasons why that year's Melbourne Games is remembered as the "Friendly Games".

Dawn of an Era

Another woman splashed onto the world stage at the 1956 Olympics. Dawn Fraser was a teenager when she won the 100-metres freestyle. She went on to claim victory in the same event at the next two Olympics, becoming the first swimmer, male or female, to achieve this. Could she have won a fourth gold in this event at the 1968 Olympics? An official ban stopped her from even trying.

Fraser was born into a family of battlers, the youngest of eight children. When she was young she would sneak into the local pool with her brothers and cling to their backs as they jumped off the high tower. It was the launch of a career that would eventually see Fraser win 8 Olympic medals, hold 39 world records, earn 6 gold at the Commonwealth Games and become the first woman to swim 100 metres in less than a minute.

Dawn Fraser taking the gold medal in the 100-metres freestyle final at the Olympic Games, Melbourne, 1956

Making Waves

Fraser broke many records. Sometimes, she also broke the rules. The Australian public loved her sense of mischief – swimming officials did not!

At the 1964 Tokyo Olympics, Fraser marched with the Australian team in the Opening Ceremony, even though the swimmers were told to rest before their events. She also chose to compete in her own swimming costume because the official swimsuit felt too tight. And then, when her races were finished, Fraser and a couple of friends tried to souvenir some of the Olympic flags that were flying near her hotel. They were caught by the police, but later allowed to go free when the superintendent realised they had arrested the Olympic champion. The superintendent also asked Fraser to pose for a photo, and gave her the stolen flag as a gift.

Banned!

Australian swimming officials were less forgiving. Months after the Tokyo Olympics, Fraser was slapped with a 10-year ban from competitive swimming. She was later told the punishment was for marching in the Opening Ceremony and for wearing an unofficial swimsuit. Whatever the reasons, this penalty was described by many as outrageous.

The ban was eventually lifted a few months before the 1968 Mexico Olympics, but by then it was too late for Fraser to prepare for the 100-metres freestyle race. It would have been a chance at a fourth gold in this event. Even today, no swimmer has won four Olympic gold medals in the same event.

Fraser did end up going to the Mexico Olympics, but as a non-competing guest. While there, a journalist challenged her to see how fast she could swim the 100 metres. It had been years since Fraser had raced and almost as long since she'd trained, but she jumped in the pool and swam the two laps in 60.2 seconds. Her time was only one-fifth of a second slower than the woman who eventually went on to win the gold medal in Mexico. What might Fraser have achieved at these Olympics had she been in proper training?

Athlete of the Century

Even without the Olympic gold from Mexico, Fraser is today recognised as Australia's greatest woman athlete, and the rest of the world agrees: in 1999 she was named World Athlete of the Century by the World Sports Awards. Fraser has also been named a National Living Treasure and was recognised internationally as one of the seven greatest Olympians of all time. Most of all, Dawn Fraser is widely loved as the person who best represents Australia's larrikin spirit.

All that Glitters is Gould

In 1972, aged fifteen, Aussie swimmer Shane Gould broke Fraser's 100-metre record on her way to becoming the fastest swimmer in the world over every freestyle distance: 100 metres, 200 metres, 400 metres, 800 metres and 1500 metres. Later that year, at the Munich Olympics, Gould won a record five individual medals, including three gold in world-record time. She retired from elite competitive swimming at seventeen. Gould did not enjoy the worldwide fame that came with her success.

Shane Gould, 1971

Mate Versus Mate

It was 1980 and the NSW rugby league team had once again beaten Queensland in the opening two matches of the interstate series. It wasn't that the northerners were bad players, even though they'd lost to NSW for the past 15 years. The trouble was that the players were chosen to represent the state in which they lived, and at that time the best talent moved to Sydney to join the top-paying competition.

With only a handful of people turning up to watch the second interstate match, an experiment was planned for the third and final game. It was based on the idea of a state of origin. This concept – in which players are selected to represent their home state, regardless of their current address – had been kicking around for years, and was usually met with a wall of opposition. Some of the doubters felt the format would lack passion because the interstate players would refuse to play hard against their regular club teammates. But league officials had no choice. A State of Origin game was organised as a last-ditch attempt to rekindle interest in interstate rugby league.

Artie Beetson looks for a teammate before passing the ball, c. 1970s

Big Artie

Thirty-five-year-old Arthur "Artie" Beetson was chosen to captain Queensland. Beetson came from Roma, west of Brisbane, and had been playing in Sydney for 15 years. He had won 2 premierships, played 14 Tests for the Australian rugby league team the Kangaroos and was the first Aboriginal captain of a national sports team. But there was one thing Artie had never done. He had never worn the maroon jersey of Queensland.

Beetson led his Maroons onto Lang Park (now Suncorp Stadium) on 8 July 1980 in front of more than 33,000 Queenslanders. From the moment the Maroons kicked off, Beetson inspired his team with powerful runs and a battery of stubborn defence. At one point Beetson stopped the NSW Blues's Mick Cronin, who had been Beetson's Parramatta Eels teammate, with a bone-crunching thwack. This tackle flattened the well-liked Cronin. This tackle also stunned the critics, who had previously said clubmates would go soft on each other in Origin games. Most of all, this tackle gave birth to the "mate versus mate, state versus state" spirit that defines Origin footy.

Beetson's role in Queensland's 20–10 victory helped unleash the State of Origin tradition. Today, Origin footy is the fiercest and most-watched rivalry on the Australian sporting calendar, with almost 100 countries around the world watching the broadcast. 1980 was the only time Beetson played State of Origin, although he coached his Queenslanders to series wins from 1982 to 1984, and again in 1989.

The Gladiators
(Norm Provan and
Arthur Summons), 1963

The Gladiators

This is the most famous photograph in rugby league. It was taken for a newspaper at the end of the 1963 grand final and shows a muddy embrace between the rival captains, St George's Norm "Sticks" Provan (left) and Western Suburbs' Arthur Summons. This picture speaks of friendship and respect, even in the toughest of sporting contests. The image was later named The Gladiators and became such a treasured symbol of mateship that it has featured on all rugby league premiership trophies since 1982.

A Yacht with Wings to Fly

The America's Cup,
c. 1900–1915

The America's Cup is the oldest trophy in the world of sport and is given to the winner of a yacht race. One of the amazing things about this regatta, which was first run in 1851, was that the New York Yacht Club had won it every time for 132 years. The sailors at this American club had defended the trophy for so long, they bolted it to their display stand with a steel rod. However, in 1983, a challenge from Down Under threatened this record-breaking winning streak.

A Western Australian man named Alan Bond had competed for the America's Cup three times and failed. But Bond had a friend, Ben Lexcen, who came up with a design for a secret winged keel that could make a yacht lighter, more stable and faster. Bond believed this yacht – named *Australia II*, with the II pronounced as the number two – could give him the technological edge he needed.

At least, that was the plan. The Australians had to beat the United States in four out of seven races. *Australia II* lost three out of the first four races because of equipment failures. If they suffered one more defeat, they would be returning home empty-handed – again. The crew refused to give up. *Australia II* overcame a false start in the fifth race to claim a comfortable win and then backed it up with another victory in the sixth race. The results were tied and, for the first time, the America's Cup was going to be decided in a final-race showdown.

Alan Bond used the famous Australian symbol of a boxing kangaroo in the flag he designed for the America's Cup challenge. Today, the boxing kangaroo is a favourite for Aussie sports fans, and is the official mascot for the Australian Olympic Team.

From a Land Down Under

Off the water, the rivalry between the nations was intense. A protective skirt was draped around *Australia II*'s winged keel so that its opponents could not see it. The mystery surrounding this design was a weapon in itself because the American sailors weren't sure what they were up against. Meanwhile, the Americans set up speakers to blast the Australians with the theme song from the boxing movie *Rocky*. The Australians replied with the song "Down Under", by the band Men at Work. The chorus of this song warned the Americans to run and take cover.

On the day of the final race, the Americans opened with a one-minute lead. But the crew on *Australia II* remained calm. Knowing they had one last chance for a comeback, they steered to the far side of the course to search for a stronger breeze.

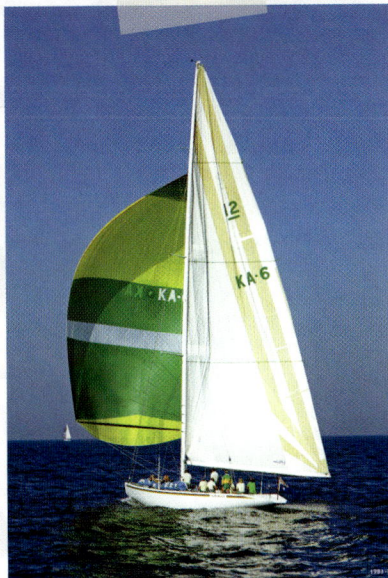

Australia II, 1983

It worked. Wind began to fill *Australia II*'s green and gold sail and it sped past its rival. The Aussies ferociously defended their lead around the final mark as the finishing line drew closer and closer. Moments later … victory.

"IT'S OURS!" announced local papers as Australians celebrated across the globe. On the east coast of the United States, Bond ordered that *Australia II* be lifted into the air to reveal its secret keel. When this happened, men in dinner suits joined hundreds who jumped into the water to get a closer look. On the other side of the world, thousands of parties formed around Australian television sets. It felt like this victory was bigger than a yacht race. The win gave Australia a sense of confidence. A little nation at the bottom of the world had brought down a giant.

I'm Black
and I'm Proud

Victoria Park is built on land that is sacred to its traditional owners, the Wurundjeri people. Prior to the European colonisation of Melbourne in the 1830s, this ancient ground was used by Aboriginal people for ceremonies, meetings and festivals. In the 1900s, the Collingwood Football Club ("The Magpies" or "The Pies") forged its own traditions at the site. The Pies turned Victoria Park into a dreaded fortress, one in which opposition teams faced not only the grit of the Magpie players but the venom of its many die-hard supporters.

"Brother, we don't have to put up with this."
GILBERT MCADAM TO NICKY WINMAR, VICTORIA PARK, 1993

Nicky Winmar, 1993

Saints and Sinners

In April 1993, Neil Elvis "Nicky" Winmar and Gilbert McAdam were at Victoria Park as members of a visiting St Kilda team ("the Saints"), two of the many talented Aboriginal players who were making a mark in Australian football. From the moment they stepped onto the field, Winmar and McAdam were hit by a storm of cruel comments from sections of the crowd. These insults were aimed, in part, at the colour of the players' skin.

The hate spewing from some in the crowd got worse when the game began. The Pies fans were especially hungry for blood because the Saints had bumped Collingwood from the finals the season before. But out on the ground, McAdam used the taunts to get fired up. He grabbed Winmar and reminded him that no one has to put up with racial abuse – not ever. "We have got to make a statement," McAdam said. And that is exactly what they did. McAdam went on to score five goals and was named "best on field". Winmar was close behind with two Brownlow votes in the Saints' first win at Victoria Park for 17 years.

When the final bell sounded, McAdam hugged the Saints fans while Winmar celebrated on the field. Then something made Winmar freeze on the spot; perhaps more mean words from members of the crowd. At that moment he turned to face the Magpie army and peeled up his jumper. Pointing to the dark skin on his body, Winmar said, "I'm black and I'm proud to be black."

Winmar's gesture was captured by two photographers and splashed across the front pages of newspapers. The image would soon become a symbol of pride for Indigenous Australians.

Celebrating Our Differences

Winmar's response came at an important time in Australia's cultural history. The Australian High Court had handed down the Mabo ruling the year before, recognising the longstanding ties of Indigenous communities to their land. In December 1992, Prime Minister Paul Keating made his landmark Redfern Speech, detailing a vision of justice and equality for Australia's Aboriginal and Torres Strait Islander populations. On top of that, 1993 was named the International Year of the World's Indigenous People. But while the winds of political change were beginning to blow, it was the image of Winmar's defiance that spoke to hearts. This stance made a statement that Indigenous Australians have a strong and proud heritage. It called for people everywhere to embrace, even celebrate, differences.

Gilbert McAdam played more than 100 Australian Football League (AFL) games before pursuing careers in coaching and the media. Nicky Winmar ended his 251-game AFL career in 1999 and has since been inducted into the West Australian Football Hall of Fame. He was one of the most naturally gifted players to ever take the field, but perhaps his greatest legacy was that moment in 1993. Two years later, the AFL brought in a rule to state that there is no place for racial abuse within the sport. Sadly, even today, this rule continues to be tested at sports fields across Australia.

Nicky Winmar, 1997

Sydney's Gold Rush

When Catherine "Cathy" Freeman was fourteen, her teacher asked her what job she wanted when she grew up. "I want to win a gold medal at the Olympic Games," Freeman replied. That moment of destiny arrived 13 years later when Freeman lined up in the 400-metres final at the Sydney Olympics.

There had been lots of reasons why Freeman found happiness in running. For starters, she wanted to make the most of her healthy arms and legs to honour her sister, Anne-Marie, who suffered from the physical disability cerebral palsy. Freeman's running was also a statement of pride in her Aboriginal heritage. One time, when she was little, Freeman won four of her five races in a regional event but the trophies were given to the non-Indigenous girls who placed second. Freeman used these experiences as a source of strength and speed.

It worked. At the 1990 Auckland Commonwealth Games, Freeman, then sixteen, was part of Australia's gold medal-winning relay team. Four years later, at the Commonwealth Games in Canada, she won gold in both the 200-metres and the 400-metres races. Freeman then won Olympic silver in the 400-metres at the 1996 Atlanta Games and followed this by winning the World Championships over the same distance in 1997 and 1999. All of this made Freeman the hot favourite for the 400 metres at the 2000 Sydney Olympics.

The Race of Our Lives

On the night of the 400-metres final, Australians everywhere stopped whatever they were doing to watch Cathy Freeman. She appeared on the Olympic track in a hooded, full-body running suit. As the runners did some last-minute stretches, more than 110,000 people around the stadium started going berserk with anticipation. Moments later the sound of the starter's gun echoed across the track and Freeman

Cathy Freeman on her way to winning the women's 400-metres final at the Sydney Olympic Games, 25 September 2000

burst from the blocks. Could she win? She was carrying the hopes of Indigenous Australians on her shoulders. She was carrying the hopes of all Australians.

Freeman was placed third as the runners sprinted out of the bend. Then she pounced. It was as if the deafening noise of the crowd lifted her off the ground and swept her across the finish line, several metres ahead of her nearest rival. Freeman had won Olympic gold! This was the dream she had held since she was a little girl, and, for the 49.11 seconds of that race, it was a dream she shared with every Australian.

The Best Ever

The 2000 Sydney Olympic Games were described as "the best ever" by the then-president of the International Olympic Committee, Juan Antonio Samaranch. Australia hosted more than 10,000 athletes from 199 nations, and won 58 medals, including 16 gold.

Seventeen-year-old swimmer Ian Thorpe led the Aussie charge with three gold and two silver medals. He would go on to claim a total of five gold, three silver and one bronze during his Olympic career, the best tally to date by an Australian.

The Flame that Unites

Cathy Freeman was given the honour of lighting the cauldron in the Opening Ceremony of the Sydney Olympics. It was a powerful statement towards reconciliation.

A hundred days earlier, the Olympic torch had begun its Australian adventure at Uluru. Nova Peris, the first Indigenous athlete to win Olympic gold (as a member of the 1996 Hockeyroos), ran in bare feet to honour the traditional owners of the land. The torch was then carried by 11,000 Australians across 27,000 kilometres, including a scuba dive on the Great Barrier Reef and an outback flight with the Royal Flying Doctor Service.

Inside the Olympic stadium, a relay of Australia's golden girls carried the torch to celebrate 100 years of women's participation in the Games, including Betty Cuthbert, Dawn Fraser, Shirley Strickland de la Hunty and Shane Gould.

Dawn Fraser, Cathy Freeman, Debbie Flintoff-King and Raelene Boyle (both Australian track champions) and Betty Cuthbert at the Opening Ceremony of the Sydney Olympic Games, 2000

A Sunburnt Country

It says a lot about our national character that Australian colonists united in sport decades before they formed a federal parliament. Many nations boast a love of sport, but in Australia, this passion defines us. Sports stars are among our greatest legends – The Don, Our Dawn, Phar Lap and the Ashes. These stories speak of our history, our values, our traditions and how we see ourselves as Australians.

More than a century has passed since James F Hogan warned that future Australians would have an excessive love of sport. We can probably guess what he would say today about our nation's enduring passion for games, scores and races. What do you think about his prediction?

Regardless of your answer, there's one thing on which we all can agree, and that is that sport has the potential to unite us. When "Australians all" rejoiced for Cathy Freeman's Olympic victory, we caught a glimpse of how rich our diverse nation can be if we share a common dream.

Sisters Booka and Chris Durack sparring with a speed bag, 1916

Glossary

ANZAC: Australian and New Zealand Army Corps.

battlers: Australian slang for a person or group of persons who persevere, even in tough times.

bicentenary: the 200th anniversary of a significant event.

bouncer: a type of delivery in cricket, usually bowled by a fast bowler, that bounces short on the pitch and rears up towards a batsman's head.

Brownlow: an annual award given to the player judged to be best and fairest in the AFL.

century: a period of 100 years, and also a score of 100 in cricket.

conscription: forced enlistment of people into the military.

diggers: a slang name for Australian soldiers.

Down Under: a nickname for Australia, referring to the nation's location in the Southern Hemisphere.

heavyweight: the heaviest weight group for a boxer.

keel: the bottom part of the boat that helps to keep it balanced and upright.

larrikin: a person with a cheeky, rowdy spirit.

Marylebone Cricket Club: the world's most famous cricket club, better known as the MCC.

middleweight: a boxing weight category that ranges in kilograms from high 60s to mid 70s.

obituary: a death notice.

paceman: a fast bowler in cricket.

pedestrianism: competitive walking or running, often professional and funded by wagering.

punter: a person who gambles, particularly on races.

reconciliation: a process of uniting to build respect and friendship between Indigenous and non-Indigenous Australians.

regatta: a series of boat races.

shirker: a person who avoids work or their duty.

Select Bibliography

Autobiographies

Bradman, Don, *Farewell to Cricket*, HarperCollins, 1994.

Cuthbert, Betty, *Golden Girl*, Strand Publishing, 2004.

Fraser, Dawn, *One Hell of a Life*, Hodder, 2001.

Freeman, Cathy, *Cathy: My Autobiography*, Highdown, 2004.

Secondary Sources

De Moore, Greg, *Tom Wills: First Wild Man of Australian Sport*, Allen & Unwin, 2008.

Fenton, Peter, *Les Darcy: The Legend of the Fighting Man*, Little Hills Press, 1995.

Johnson, Len, *The Landy Era*, Melbourne Books, 2009.

Klugman, Matthew and Osmond, Gary, *Black and Proud: The Story of an Iconic AFL photo*, NewSouth Publishing, 2013.

Documentaries

Bradman: Centenary Collection (ABC)

Phar Lap: The People's Champion (Raceplay)

Websites

Australian Olympic Committee: www.corporate.olympics.com.au

National Sports Museum: www.nsm.org.au

Sport Australia Hall of Fame: www.sahof.org.au

Index